Blessings *from* Nature

Simple & Short Poems
that will inspire you

Pooja Sharma

Thank you mom & dad for everything

Preface

The word *'alchemy'* has always fascinated me. I remember during the pandemic, I suffered a lot from overthinking. I would repeatedly have negative thoughts running through my head all day long. I would often wonder, "How can I *'alchemize'* this? How can I use this negative pattern in a positive fashion? Is that even possible?"

It was then that I thought, I bet poetry requires constant repetition of thoughts, words, lines, and rhymes. Why not give it a go? I would go for long walks with my dog and repeat the same lines/words to come up with rhymes for my poems.

We can *'alchemize'* almost anything; it is our superpower.

All poems in this book are centered around elements of nature. They are written from their unique perspective. These poems will make you feel nostalgic, happy, and leave you with a childlike wonder for life.

Blessings are all around us; sometimes, we forget how lucky we truly are to be alive and breathing on our mother planet. My idea behind writing poetry was to express deep thoughts using the simplest of words in the shortest way possible. I wanted the afterthought to be grand, even if the poems were short. Please note: All poems are written from the perspective of nature and its elements; it is like nature reciting poetry to the reader.

Moreover, I am a Chemical Engineer from NIT Jaipur. I am a Senior Analyst at American Express. I am also a part-time musician.

I love animals,

I love nature,

I love most things :)

I hope you enjoy this book.

Here's a piece of my heart for all you wonderful readers~

Contents

Contents

• • •

Wind

i swoosh through forests

i whoosh through plains

i swirl the clouds

i twirl the rains

i tickle the roses

i ripple the seas

i am the scent

the good earth breathes~

Isn't it wonderful...that the wind picks the most beautiful parts of everything it touches?

Pond

like i show the sky,

its beauty from afar,

can i please show you

how beautiful you are? :)

Oh, to be a sweet little pond...reflecting the blue sky on a sunny day...

When you see beauty in the world, reflect it back.

Lotus

do not reduce yourself
to your surroundings,
even with dirt around,
you can bloom, darlings!

When life throws dirt at you, don't forget to bloom!

Sunflower

i look like a little sun,

vibrant flames of yellow,

i wish to light up this world,

like the mighty fellow!

If we become who we think we are...then why not aspire to be magical, mystical creatures?

Firefly

don't be afraid of the dark,

let me illuminate the night,

i can guide you on the path,

like a flickering fairy light! ✨

Even a flicker of light has the power to dispel darkness...just a little bit is enough~

Honeybee

i forage for some flower juice,

i save it for when it gets cold,

like a shimmering alchemist,

i turn it into liquid gold!

With patience and hard work, we can learn to alchemize anything.

Oasis

from a magical land,

a ruby in the sand,

a tropical dream,

i appear to be

all the mystical dunes,

a mirage of monsoons,

a golden haven,

the desert and me.

Without the desert, the oasis would just be a puddle.

Sometimes, it is the existence of hardships and challenges that make something extraordinarily beautiful~

Cloud

what do you observe

when you look at me,

a puff of vanilla mist

or fluff of cotton candy?

some see a bear

some see a swan,

whoever doodled me

fancied a white crayon!

Imagination and reality are a beautiful mix~

Butterfly

when i was a small caterpillar,

i didn't possess a set of wings,

but with patience & perseverance,

you can transform into many things!

Perseverance is no less than a superpower. With great practice comes the power of transformation~

Green Plants

come to my mess,

it's a beautiful day,

pass me some sun,

read the menu today

we cook non-stop,

it's a lovely buffet,

we make life juice,

sip! sip! sip it away!

Sip on the fresh juice at the garden party of life. What a wonderful world~

Sun

when you have a pot of gold,

you do not hide it away,

"share your wealth" i was told,

let's do that everyday!

If the Sun didn't share its light, there would be no life on Earth.

Don't forget to share your light with those who really need it.

Moon

i must be the moon,
nightlight of the skies,
i pick a bit of sunshine
and silver the lullabies~

Even on the darkest of nights, the moon turns its light on and shines through.

It's inspiring, isn't it?

Shooting Star

today's your lucky day
ask for a thing or two
i'll take a mighty fall
to make your wish come true!

Sometimes, the whole universe conspires to make your wish come true, so be sure to ask for the right thing at the right time.

Sky

i spin the golden pot,

i pin the silver dot,

i shun the glitter box

in jewels of sundown

i pick shiny stars,

i stick ruby mars,

i tuck tiny gems

in little earth's crown!

The night sky looks like a giant scrapbook with glitters and stars. Whoever designed our universe must've been a meticulous artist!

Oyster

i keep my mansion clean,

i lock the entrance first,

when the dirt barges in,

i mock pearls out of dust!

You have the power to turn any bad thought that enters your mind into a pearl simply by choosing how to react to it. The power is yours.

Bird

the world is your oyster,

let's have some fun today,

a brand new adventure,

is just a flight away!

Sometimes, taking a leap of faith can lead to an adventure of a lifetime!

Summer

warm toned skies,
dried corn fields,
hot baked earth,
sun kissed dreams,

purple cherry wine,
yellow lemon trees,
gypsy butterflies,
tipsy honey bees,

fresh mango scent,
cool ocean breeze,
rich summer gold,
sweet treasuries

Why chase fool's gold when you have an abundance of sweet summer treasure?

Rain

i wash all dust away,

i sprinkle fresh and new,

flowers bloom in the rain,

no reason you can't too!

When it starts to rain, you may feel like you are drowning, but always remember—it is essential for the bloom!

Blackhole

a bit of theatre
in the ebony skies,
cue a supernova
i'm about to arrive,

i feast like a monster
on stars and asteroids,
a beast of astral realm
spitting fire in the void!

There will be monsters lurking in the dark...but don't be scared. Accept them as a part of life and keep moving ahead.

Forest

whistling winds,

chirping crickets,

babbling brooks,

as they cue along

take a seat,

the orchestra,

will play you a

sensational song!

There is no bigger showman than nature itself. Always show up to experience its greatness!

Nature

under the rose-tinted skies,

i pour blue water into lakes,

scented flowers everywhere,

i'm the gardener of this place!

The magic of reality can be better than fiction sometimes.

Animal Kingdom

a big blue-blooded octopus,
a round red hippopotamus

a bullet-proof armadillo,
a kangaroo with a pillow

a roly-poly panda bear,
a silky-milky pony mare

a cuddly-bubbly elephant,
a squirrel with a nutty scent

a fuzzy-buzzy honeybee,

a dolphin whistling at the sea

a chubby-tubby polar bear,

a whisky-frisky woolly hare

a moony-toony owly hoot,

a penguin in a raincoat suit

a planet full of mystic beings,

a true magician trick it seems!

Don't you find it strange when people don't believe in magic? Every living creature around us looks so different, and somehow, we all live under the same blue sky. Now that's real magic!

Autumn

i'm not petrified of change,

it occurs for good reason,

i roll out the red carpet

to welcome a new season!

Change is difficult. It is out of our comfort zone. However, just like autumn, we can learn to not only accept but also embrace change~

Spring

i'm a little flamboyant,

how about a vibrant look?

throw some paint on the landscape,

like it's a colouring book!

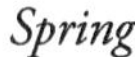

Just like spring, when things get dull, throw some colours on the canvas of life!

Winter

the land is baked,

i'll get some icing,

let's decorate for

festive reasons,

sweet snow frosting,

sprinkled all around,

enjoy the dessert

of all seasons!

Even the coldest season of life is sure to bring some sweetness along!

www.ingramcontent.com/pod-product-compliance
Lightning Source LLC
Chambersburg PA
CBHW040915110726
48005CB00006B/904